T0368486

# BECOME COLOR CONSCIOUS

## AND TRANSFORM YOUR EXPERIENCES

LIEN POTGIETER

Balboa Press books may be ordered through booksellers or by contacting:

Balboa Press
A Division of Hay House
1663 Liberty Drive
Bloomington, IN 47403
www.balboapress.com
1 (877) 407-4847

ISBN: 978-1-5043-8601-2 (sc)
ISBN: 978-1-5043-8602-9 (e)

The Library of Congress Control Number: 2017912665

Print information available on the last page.

Balboa Press rev. date: 01/09/2018

BALBOA
PRESS
A DIVISION OF HAY HOUSE

# Foreword

Dearest Color Lover

I am over the moon that you have taken to bold step to invest in this workbook and your color consciousness. When you have completed all the fun, interactive activities, you will see yourself and the world through different eyes. You will be fully aware of the magical effect that color has on your well-being.

My first wish is that you become color conscious. By learning to speak this magical language you will expand your awareness and live a happier and healthier life.

My second wish is that you start noticing the small miracles that happen around you every day; that you find the beauty and color in everything and everyone you meet, and inspire others to do the same.

Remember, it is all about your own experience with color, so like with everything in life – the more you put in, the more you can expect the magic of color to reflect back at you.

Colorful blessings

Lien

# Contents

# 1 – How this book works

This workbook will become like a close friend with whom you share everything about your color conscious journey.

Write down as much as you can. You'll find the more you do, the more you awaken to the change color is having in your life and the magic starts flowing!

In every chapter you will have activities to complete – any thoughts or reflections, ideas or inspirations that come up during the activity can be recorded in your book. By the end you should have your own personalised, color conscious notes. Set aside about an hour each day for your new awareness activities.

At the end of this book, I would love you to add it to your coffee table collection. Share it with friends and never be shy to show your true colors.

# 2 – Spiritual and material stuff you need to succeed

Before we start the hard but rewarding work of becoming color conscious, you should know what attitude is needed to succeed.

On the spiritual plane, you must have:

- A love of beauty
- Unstoppable curiosity
- An open mind
- A genuine interest in living a happier, healthier, more conscious life
- An adventurous spirit

On the material plane, you must have:

- Lots of colored crayons, pens, and pencils
- An hour per day dedicated time

# 3 – How color aware are you?

*A wise person once said: Flowers are the earth's way of smiling.*

I say, color is earth and heaven's way to show us that there is more to life than mere existing.

Color – like love, wonder and miracles – is all around. It is in our homes, our clothes, our food, nature and even in our speech. Have you ever been red with rage, or green with envy?

However, most of us live such a fast paced life that we hardly notice all the colorful things around us.

Over the next five chapters you'll be *exploring your own awareness of color.* Open your mind, your senses, your heart, and enjoy!

## Color activity 1

Your first task is to take a picture of yourself – no frills, just as you are right now!

If you are feeling more creative, take time to create an artistic impression of yourself. Use anything you desire – paints, pencils, colored paper, crayons, glitter, chalk, colored pens, pastels, stickers – be bold! You are a kaleidoscope of thoughts, feelings, experiences, talents and connections so give yourself permission to express them all!

*Create your selfie here:*

Take some time to reflect on your picture and creation. Do certain colors come to mind or stand out? As what color would you describe yourself? Do you feel you could use a certain color for balance, or are there colors missing from your pictures?

- Keep your picture and artistic creation for the end of the journey. You'll be re-doing them after reading this entire book. Be prepared to be surprised by the change!

# Color activity 2

So let's see how color aware you really are… Write down as many colors you can think of.

_____

_____

_____

How well did you do?

I am guessing you missed a few!

Were you surprised at how many colors there actually are? If you Google "color palette" you'll find there are masses of color spectrums, and more colors then you probably ever imagined.

Color is all around us in ABUNDANCE, but most of us limit our minds to the basics we know: red, yellow, blue! If we are willing to open our minds, drop the limitations and really look, we see that there is so much more possibility (think fuscia, emerald, mustard, chartreause).

And this is not just in color, but in every aspect of our interaction with the world.

# Color activity 3

To help identify the feelings you associated with the different colors, match the different FEELINGS below to the COLORS you associate them with:

| Red | Compassion | Serious |
|---|---|---|
| Green | Passion | Sad |
| Blue | Aggression | Powerful |
| Pink | Repressed | Isolated |
| Yellow | Optimistic | Comforting |
| Gold | Jealous | Energized |
| Black | Peaceful | Forgiving |
| Orange | Fearful | Understanding |
| White | Joy | Safe |
| Brown | Happy | Stuck |
| Grey | Indecisive | Encouraged |

How do your answers compare to these?

| Red | Passion | Aggression |
|---|---|---|
| Green | Compassion | Jealous |
| Blue | Sad | Peaceful |
| Pink | Forgiving | Energized |
| Yellow | Optimistic | Happy |
| Gold | Understanding | Powerful |
| Black | Safe | Stuck |
| Orange | Joy | Encouraged |
| White | Clarity | Sad |
| Brown | Serious | Repressed |
| Grey | Critical | Isolated |

You probably didn't get the match up exactly the same as this one but it's ok, it wasn't really a test.

As you work through this book you will receive information linked to each color. Remember these are just guidelines. We each have a personal association with different colors and it's important to trust that, so you formulate your own unique relationship with color and make it work for you.

Color teaches us that with anything in life, the most important thing is to trust your own feelings, wisdom, and guidance.

# Color activity 4

For the final fun with color today, here's a five-minute (or less) visualization to do.

- Make sure you are sitting comfortably and relaxed, in a quiet space.
- Take a few deep breathes in and out, focusing on your breath so you quiet your mind.
- Imagine yourself in a big, protective white bubble.
- Focus on your heart and try connecting to what you FEEL (really let yourself feel it, not what your mind thinks you should feel).
- Now bring in any color – go with the first color that comes to mind without too much thought. This will be your intuition speaking and the perfect color for you to connect to in this moment.
- Imagine you are being showered with this color, so it fills your whole body and bubble. Spend some time breathing in the color.
- When you feel full-up on the color, become aware of your heart again and connect to what you are feeling now.

How did your feelings or mood change after this activity?
_____

_____

Was it easy to connect to a color?
_____

_____

What color came through for you (maybe it was a new color from the color palette… periwinkle, banana?)
_____

_____

What do you associate with this color?
_____

_____

Color is a natural healer, and as I hope you learnt from this visualization, is a simple, natural, fun way to help you enhance your mood and feel more balanced. Plus it is free and available to you any time. All you need to do is to take a few minutes to tap into your own imagination and intuition.

# 4 – Clothes and homes

Before you get up (if you are connecting with color first thing in the morning, which is a great idea by the way) or start reading, try this:

- Connect to your heart (exactly as you did in the visualization activity in the previous chapter – remember – sit quietly, focus on your breath, put yourself in a protective bubble, and then focus on your HEART).
- For about five minutes, focus on your heart and really try connect to your feelings. Just sit and become the observer of anything that comes up – make a note of any feelings that come up for you.
- When you're done, without thinking too much about it, you're going to get dressed in whatever item of clothing in your cupboard catches your eye first, or what you are most drawn to.
- Once you're dressed, you can go back to your heart. Spend a few minutes connecting as you did before, and again observe what feelings or emotions come up for you. Make a note of them here:

_____

_____

_____

_____

_____

_____

_____

_____

_____

_____

This chapter is all about your personal preferences for color.

Have you ever wondered why rock stars traditionally always dress in black? Or why friends might wear bright, bold colors that get you pulling out your sunglasses, and that you would rather run from?

Although many people are sceptics about color affecting our behaviours and moods, a journey with this book means diving into your own color psychology and exploring what's real for you.

Today it's all about your clothes and homes – the colors directly around you and chosen by you.

# Color activity 1

By now you should have completed the "getting dressed" activity shared with you at the beginning of the chapter.

---

**How did it go?**

What feelings and emotions came up or did you experience before you got dressed?

_____

_____

What color did you get dressed in? Do you always wear this color?

_____

_____

Did you notice specific color trends in your cupboard? Are you aware of a specific range of colors you always choose to wear?

_____

_____

What did you experience once you got dressed? Did your feelings change? Did you feel different?

_____

_____

Did the color you chose to wear reflect your self-expression in that moment?

_____

_____

---

I hope you noticed a difference once you were dressed.

The colors we are drawn to wear can reflect our identity and self-expression. For example, a preference for **black** can signify mystery, secrecy and revolting against norms (matches those rock star stereo-types!), but it is also known to have a healing property of protection. How convenient, considering the masses of fans that celebrities must contend with wherever they go.

A preference for red is associated with great energy and action, and also has a healing property of increased energy levels. Have you ever noticed the predominant color soccer teams wear? (Just saying, but I haven't ever noticed a lot of green, which is associated with harmony, calmness, and balance.)

Although we are not always fully conscious of it, the colors we choose to wear can be significant. They help us express ourselves, and can also heal us at the same time. The more we allow our intuition to guide us in using color (by connecting to the heart and acting from instinct as you did in choosing your outfit this morning), the more we open opportunity for the magic of color to work in all aspects of our lives.

*The heart is a magical intelligence that can always whisper the secret to anything you need to know.*

The short activity of connecting to your heart is one way you can always connect to your intuition – not just when you are working with color. Use it any time you feel overwhelmed, confused, stuck, or need to make a decision. The intuition always knows what to do next!

## Color activity 2

For the rest of this chapter, spend time observing the different colors people around you are wearing. Make notes of colors that you don't like at all and would never wear, and also colors you like, or would like to wear but don't have in your cupboard.

## Color activity 3

What colors surround you in your home or at work? Coral, periwinkle, emerald, cobalt? Remember the color spectrum from the previous chapter? Think beyond the norm when you try naming them!

_____

_____

_____

Spend a few minutes in each room in your home or work, absorb the predominant colors and become aware of how they affect you.

What feelings do you associate with each room based on the color?

_____

_____

How does each room make you feel?

_____

_____

What happens to your body – do you relax, tense, feel energised, maybe start feeling hungry?

_____

_____

Or do you want to just get up and dance, sing and express yourself? (If so… please do, no-one's watching.)

_____

_____

If you like, take a picture of or draw your own pictures of the space you work and live in.

Using different colors in your home is just another way you can make color work for you. In general, red, orange, and yellow are warm exciting and alive colors, so will tend to energise. Cooler colors such as blues, greens and purples are more calming and create the illusion of spaciousness. So if you struggle with something like insomnia, you might benefit from changing your room color – just say no to the red.

# Color activity 4

Now that you are aware of how the colors in your home affect you it is time to create and decorate your chill space, your creative place, or your me room. Decide on the colors of the wall, then add the furniture, curtains, and accessories in the colors that inspire you, motivate you, relax you or make you feel safe and loved.

# 5 – Food for thought

Food glorious food – in the color world, it's not all just about taste sensations.

Today get ready to have your mouth watering as it's all about awakening to color and food.

Food is one of the most effective ways to incorporate color into your life. Apart from the joy and fun of it all, different colored foods affect the way we feel.

The color energy of the food we eat resonates with the physical, emotional, mental, or spiritual energy that we need.

So there's more to those chocolate cravings after all.

## Color activity 1

Firstly, throughout the day, become aware of the different colors of the foods you are eating.

Choose one specific food that you are drawn to because of its color and spend time eating it mindfully. Pay attention to the way your body responds to it, to the different sensations in your body, to your mood and emotions.

** If you don't have access to lots of different food throughout your day, you can also try this by just paging through different magazines and pull out pictures of different colored foods that jump out at you.

For fun and to help get you started, match these foods to the emotional, mental or spiritual energy you think they provide, based on their color:

| Food | Benefit |
|---|---|
| Tomatoes | Concentration |
| Pumpkin | Balance |
| Cheese | Stamina |
| Avocado | Relaxation |
| Beetroot | Pain relief |
| Honey | Motivation |
| Olives | Stimulates intellect |

Have you ever considered the color of food before?

_____

_____

Are you aware of being drawn to certain colored foods? If yes, which colors?

_____

_____

What are the colors of the food you are eating most often?

_____

_____

And now, your very own Color Chef challenge…

**… to make the most color-conscious meal possible for the day.**

Your colorful food creation has to represent all it means to be color conscious – happy, inspirational, beautiful and of course, FULL of color (healthy is optional).

Take a picture of your creation and paste it here, or draw a picture. You can name it if you choose.

I hope this chapter has helped you understand the power of color in food. It not only adds joy and fun to the experience of eating, but has amazing healing effects too.

If we look beyond the obvious, we can also notice the subtleties of this magic in nature, especially with changing seasons. As winter begins, we need warmth and comfort. The bright orange of citrus fruits is suddenly everywhere if we are aware, providing natural warmth and joy when we need it most, plus the added vitamin C. The more we are attuned to nature and the natural foods that abound in each season, the easier it is to see that food color is not just a coincidence and can be one of the most beautiful, natural well-being agents around.

For the next chapter, you need to keep your smart phone handy and be open to some sun chasing (no selfies involved)!

Find a place to soak up a sunrise or sunset over the next day – using all five senses. Print and stick your picture in your workbook.

# 6 – Color and your senses

I see, hear, taste, feel, and smell color!

As we awaken to its essence, we can see it is possible to absorb and experience color from all five senses. There's no better way to do this then to play with nature and music.

When last did you touch and feel the velvet of rose petals, hear colorful birds singing or smell the greenness of grass? When listening to music, can you feel or hear its color?

Today is your chance to experiment!

## Color activity 1

Go on a scavenger hunt of your garden or a nearby park. Make a list of all the colors you see and take pictures of colorful flowers, trees, shrubs, leaves, plants, fish, butterflies, and birds. Become aware of the magnitude of color in nature.

Are you normally aware of so many different colors in nature?

_____

_____

How did you feel as you connected with the nature images and multitude of colors?

_____

_____

What senses were stimulated?

_____

_____

Write something about this experience of connecting to nature and its natural abundance of color. It could be a poem, a paragraph, or just a sentence.

_____

_____

_____

# Color activity 2

By now I hope you've had chance to soak up that sunset or sunrise.

We have the opportunity to see sunsets and sunrises all the time, but do you ever take the time to fully see and appreciate such a simple moment?

Have a look at your picture and count the number of colors you can see and write it down.

Everyday nature reveals an ever-changing, natural artistic color creation – and it's freely available, for anyone, anytime. Think of it as the universes very own art experiment!

I hope this stood out for you from the sunset/sunrise pictures. If we take time to be in nature and really "see" its colors and the vast beauty and diversity it provides, the world becomes a fun, colorful playground! Add in all five senses and you can never be bored.

Nature also teaches us the value of gratitude for the small, simple things. Even in the darkest, scariest moments, we can choose to look up, soak in some natural beauty and see that every day is full of color no matter what we are going through. It may give some comfort to know that as nature is always changing its colors, our own emotional states will naturally change too.

So next time you are feeling a little dull, down, or just need some inspiration – one dose of sunset for you. Just think of the beauty and healing freely available, with all its warm, radiating, joyful colors.

# Color activity 3

Music time!

The association between music and color has been studied around the globe. The general findings confirm there is a link between music and color, with upbeat music being associated with warm, bright colors and more tearful, sad music associated with cooler, dark, dull colors. So it's normally the emotion behind the music that links us to a certain color.

Find and listen to the following songs. As you do, make notes of the colors the music brings to mind. Also note the feelings or emotions you are associating with the color through the music.

Colorful – The Parlotones

I see fire – Ed Sheeren

Come into the light – Bliss

Fade to black – Metalicca

Ludwig van Beethoven - Für Elise

What colors came to mind? Can you give each song a color?

_____

_____

_____

What feelings or emotions did you associate with each?

_____

_____

_____

Have you ever associated music with color before?

_____

_____

Does this change the way you listen to music, or associate with color?

_____

_____

# 7 – Color and marketing

Did you know it takes on average 90 seconds for a customer to form an opinion about a product, and 62% to 90% of that interaction is determined by the color of the product?

Did you know 85% of the reason you buy a specific product has to do with its color?

That's according to some research.

For our last chapter of awakening to color we are thinking big brands, colorful logos and website design. We are going to explore and do our own research around color in marketing and branding.

So be prepared for some changes to your shopping experiences!

## Color activity 1

Some branding fun.

Can you guess the well-known brands these colors represent?

_____  _____  _____  _____

There is a lot of research available on color psychology, especially as it is used in branding and website design.

Here are a few more tips that you can find:

- If you're marketing to men focus on blues, greens and black, and stay away from purple, orange and brown.
- In terms of marketing, female color preferences are blue, purple, and green, and stay away from orange, brown, and grey.
- Blue is one of the most used colors on websites – it resonates trust, peace and loyalty (consider the world's biggest social network is blue – a company with core values of transparency and trust).
- Using green helps with the 'isolation effect' – when you want something to stand out because it needs to be remembered.
- Orange can be associated with fun and togetherness and can bring attention to something if used in marketing, but can also be overwhelming if used too much so the message could be lost.

- Darker tones like **black** are associated with luxury products and services.
- Bright colors are used for anything that has a call to action and have the highest conversion rates.
- Too many colors used in branding and marketing can create a sense of confusion.

## Color activity 2

Spend some time looking at different websites of well-known brands, or scroll through magazines to become aware of the colors used.

Try the heart connection exercise as you do this so you actually *feel* how the different colors are affecting you.

You can also do some of your own internet research on color psychology and branding.

Were you able to pick up any trends in the way color is being used for marketing and branding?

_____

_____

_____

Was there anything specific that stood out for you?

_____

_____

_____

If you have your own brand, will you adjust the coloring after this?

_____

_____

_____

Which company websites were you drawn to? Why?

_____

_____

_____

So are you ready to re-design your website or create your own personal brand after this?

# Color activity 3

It is time to design your own logo! Think carefully about how you want to present yourself to the world in terms of color. Now take your name and surname, come up with a title or slogan, choose your color and design your brand identity.

It is amazing how impactful color is on our psyche. As color conscious beings, we can use color to help our own businesses or creative pursuits. And hopefully we also have insight as to where we are buying things not because they make our heart sing, but because a clever color conscious individual was behind the branding and marketing!

# Color activity 4

How was your awareness of color changed over the last five days?

Have a look back through your notes so far and make a mind map of all the different colors you have connected with and the emotions and qualities you associate with each one.

My color mind map:

I hope that over the last five days you have awakened to the magic and potential of color, which is everywhere. My wish is that you are already experiencing its effects and having a happier, more joyful and fun every day experience because of it.

In the next two chapters, we look at the science of color and then your color personality, before we dive into each color individually.

In preparation I'll leave you with the thought… if you had to be a color, what color would you be?

_____

# 8 – Science of color

"The truth is the power of color is the very essence of life."

For the scientific minds, today we explore a small part of the science of color.

Thanks to the famous minds of Aristotle and Newton we can understand exactly where color comes from and how it can have such power in this world.

And as any color conscious individual knows, we never forget the play! Along with some science you'll get to have fun with all the basics any artist would know about color, so enjoy.

Light is the most important energy source for us in this world.

Our main source of light, the sun, transmits this energy through different wavelengths and frequencies (we know this thanks to Aristotle way back, around 384 BC – 322 BC).

All the frequencies of light we need to exist on earth are known as the electromagnetic spectrum.

Visible light, in the centre of the spectrum, is the only light we can see with the human eye and is how we see color (and this is thanks to Isaac Newton, who discovered the seven rainbow colors when he passed sunlight through a glass prism back in the 1600s).

**For fun**

Do you remember the color spectrum or rainbow order from school days? Test yourself!

Move these colors around so you create a color spectrum in the correct order:

Check yourself against this one:

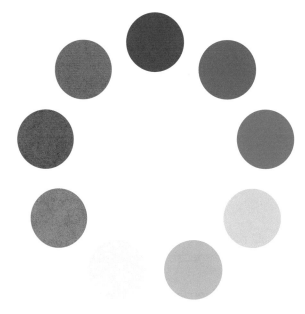

We can see this because when the visible spectrum light rays touch an object, the different frequencies are absorbed and then reflected back as color.

So each color has its own frequency.

As human beings, we each have our own frequency too. Our individual frequencies have a unique, natural state of balance. We heal through color by absorbing the frequencies we need to keep us in our own state of balance. So it's magic and science at play!

**For fun, here's some more color insight you might have forgotten from school art days.**

* There are only three primary colors.

* Secondary colors are formed by combining two primary colors 50-50.

Move the colors around to form a table that shows what the three secondary colors (green, orange, and purple) and made up of.

|  |  |  |  |
|---|---|---|---|
|  | ● | = | ● |
|  | ● | = | ● |
| ● | ● | = | ● |

* Tertiary colors are formed by combining a primary and secondary color. Work out the different colors below.

Red and orange    =    _____

Yellow and orange  =    _____

Yellow and green    =    _____

Blue and green      =    _____

Blue and purple     =    _____

Red and purple      =    _____

* Complementary colors are opposite each other on the color wheel and will create balance when used together.

* And finally, tints and shades! A color becomes a tint when white is added to it, and a shade when black is added to it.

Creativity is our natural essence. Working through this color fun is not about making you an artist. It's about enhancing your journey into color and stimulating your own natural, colorful, creative energy. The more we get into and allow ourselves to 'play' (like creating your own color wheel), the more we can access the part of ourselves that is the endless creative being, here to enjoy and play in this colorful world.

# 9 – Your color personality

Have you been thinking about what color you are?

In this exciting chapter, you will discover your color personality!

The color you are most attracted to in the long run is called your color identity and it can reveal things about your physical and mental states. You can also add all the numbers of your birth date and reduce it to one digit. For example, 12 July 1974 = 1 + 2 + 7 + 1 + 9 + 7 + 4 = 31. 3 + 1 = 4. If you are a 4, your color personality is green.

Of course the personality descriptions are in general, as we can be such multi-dimensional, complex beings. But it's another fun way to explore your own consciousness.

With which color do you most identify? What is the color of your heart?

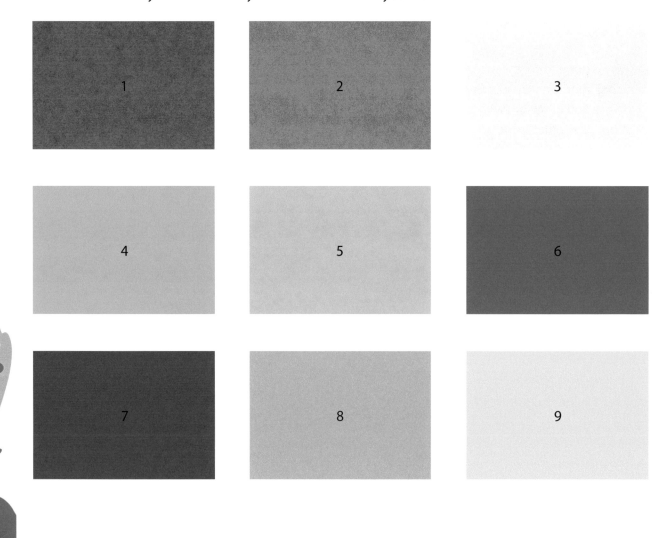

**RED/1**

If you are full of energy, passionate and physically active you are a RED person. Outgoing, motivated and determined are words used to describe you. The other side is that RED people tend to be stubborn and may have a short temper. RED personalities are also associated with impulsiveness, sexiness and a will to win. They want to live life to the full, but can have too much going on in their lives. If you identify with red you could benefit from wearing turquoise to balance you.

**ORANGE/2**

If you would describe yourself as practical and spontaneous you are ORANGE. You are creative and enjoy being in a job that requires you to be active. Your body is full of positive emotions but you can also stress too much. Other words that can describe someone with an orange identity or personality include sociable, outgoing, confident and hasty. Connecting to or wearing light blue will help in balancing if you identify with orange.

**YELLOW/3**

Sunny, warm and an inspiration to others would make you a YELLOW. You think a lot and often have a scientific mind. Yellows can also be ambitious and eager to please, but tend to live a care-free life. Other words to describe a yellow identity include co-ordinated, domineering, intellectual and courageous. As a yellow personality, remember to eat healthily because you tend to forget about food.

**GREEN/4**

If you identity with GREEN and are in balance, you can be described as conscientious, harmonious, understanding, contented, cautious, reserved and tidy. You strive for balance and harmony, are curious and compassionate by nature, and love to learn new things. The balance color for you to identify with is purple.

**BLUE/5**

BLUE people are gentle and peaceful. They are introverts and don't like conflict. BLUE people are good listeners and sensitive. Others feel comfortable in their space and they are a good judge of character. They are also easily hurt and seek stable relationships without conflict. Be careful not to isolate yourself, and remember to communicate your needs. A good color to balance you would be orange or yellow.

**INDIGO/6**

Connected to your intuition? Then you are an INDIGO person. You need tranquil surroundings and love to be surrounded by beauty. People would describe you as loyal and discerning. You are not always right though. Asking questions will help to rectify wrong perceptions.

**PURPLE/7**

Sensitive and easily hurt? Like to be surrounded by caring, compassionate people? Then you are VIOLET. You are also artistic and highly intuitive. Just take care not to get affected to other people's energies. Other words to describe the purple identity are individualistic, disorganised, self-respecting, visionary, doubting, spiritual, peaceful and calm. Green is a great balancing color for you.

If you have identified with SILVER the most, it means a restless and insecure personality. You need to feel safe, and seek secure environments to make home. As a silver personality, you can be quite serious in nature and repress your emotions. Connecting to bright, bold colors will help with balancing.

Associating with GOLD as your color identify means independence, self-control and self-reliance, and is also the color of non-commitment. You can swing with opinions and emotions and will tend to be the observer in a group. Be care not to self-criticize if this is your color.

# Color activity 1

How did the description resonate with you?

_____

_____

Could you identify with some of the traits of your color personality?

_____

_____

If you didn't, is there another description that suits you better? Does that color resonate with you?

_____

_____

Continue playing with the idea of color personality throughout the day. Think about different friends or family members and guess which color they would be. You can get their input and see how closely your guess matches up and have fun discussing it.

Think why they are that quality, what makes them that color and what qualities stand out linked to that color.

Using the color personality and identity can be a fun way to connect with ourselves and others, and opens a door to see ourselves in a new light.

How did the color personality profiling go with your friends and family? Were you able to get the colors right?

_____

_____

I hope you missed a few just because it highlights an important lesson: The idea of stereo-typing. We so easily put things in boxes, especially people, and even color. But if we are aware of that we can choose to change it. As we allow ourselves to see people and the world with an open mind and loving heart, we stand to be amazed at the possibilities, wonder and mystery every interaction can hold.

In the next ten chapters, we'll be focusing on one color per chapter. At the start of each chapter you'll receive a page with insight about the color and its properties and uses. This will include its healing properties, mental and emotional connections, meanings of preferences and aversions, home uses, energy centers and corresponding fragrances. You'll also have one activity to do that helps you connect to the color on a deeper level.

It's always good to express your experience, as it makes it more real and long-lasting in your own consciousness so you're more likely to change.

**Warning:** Color is contagious, so be prepared for more happy, healthy changes.

At the end of the chapter share your experience with the color. Even one word is cool, for example Red = Radical!

# 10 – Fiery red

Today is a day for passion, energy, support, activity and grounding – as we connect to **FIERY RED.**

## Red activity

By now you should be dressed in your fiery red outfit, feeling energised and ready for an active and power-filled day!

Throughout the day, try and notice how you feel wearing red, especially if you do any exercise.

What emotions did you connect to wearing red?

_____

_____

Did you feel more balanced/unbalanced?

_____

_____

Did you feel any different throughout the day?

_____

_____

Was there a change in your energy levels? Did you feel more present or focused?

_____

_____

Were you attracted to the red, or did you avoid wearing it?

_____

_____

Did people react differently to you wearing read?

_____

_____

**Red color quote to leave you with for the day**

Red protects itself. No color is as territorial. It stakes a claim, is on the alert against the spectrum. - Derek Jarman

**Red is generally associated with the following emotions and state of being**

**Balanced:** Grounding; strengthening; stimulating; stability; security; physical sexuality; courage; activity; passion; power; safety; warmth.

**Unbalanced**: Dominant; quick tempered; aggressive; angry; impatient.

**Red has the following physical and emotional healing properties**

Brings warmth, energy and stimulation to the whole body; energises all organs.

Energises heart and blood circulation, builds up blood, causes haemoglobin to multiply and raises blood pressure.

Good for fatigue and colds.

Stimulates ovulation and menstruation and increases sexual drive.

Causes adrenal glands to release adrenalin resulting in increased strength.

Helps loosen stiff area in the body.

Helps stimulate passion and motivation.

Keeps one grounded; connects one to the physical body.

**Red is not helpful**

When you are angry, irritable and impatient.

When you suffer from high blood pressure, heart conditions, asthma, and epilepsy.

**Use red in your home**

In rooms where you are physically active, for example playrooms.

Can result in restlessness or insomnia if used in a bedroom.

Can make a space look smaller and claustrophobic, but if used well can make it warm and cosy.

Draws people together and stimulates conversation.

**Red affirmations to be repeated often to help you through challenges**

I have courage; I feel alive; I have a right to be here.

**Foods**

Red apples, tomatoes, cherries, radishes, red cabbage, strawberries, cloves, Vitamin B, Vitamin E, Iron, and Vitamin C.

**Wear red to**

Project an air of vitality and energy.

Emphasise your spirit of independence and individuality.

Too much could be projected as aggression and dominance.

**Chakra link**

Associated with the root/base chakra (base of spine): The seat of life-force and energy.

**Fragrances and crystals**

Clary Sage; Rosemary

Garnet, Jasper, Aventurine

**Preferences and aversions**

A preference for red can signify temperamental and ambitious people; a need for personal freedom; great energy, impulse, action, assertiveness, aggression, courage and power.

An aversion to red can signify difficulties with other people who are aggressive, ego-centric and hot-tempered; hidden fears or rejection of your own assertiveness.

# 11 – Joyful orange

JOYFUL ORANGE should stimulate your creative juices and have you out and about, connecting and having fun.

Orange activity

Since it's all about creative fun, your challenge today is to take a picture of the most creative display of orange you can find (or create yourself). If you need some inspiration, remember nature is an instant canvas of creativeness.

Are you thinking fields of pumpkins? Thought so!

How did orange feel to you?

_____

_____

Was it warm, cold, excited, tearful?

_____

_____

Did you feel any change in your creativity on having to connect to the color?

_____

_____

Were you inspired by anything?

_____

_____

Orange inspiration to leave you with for the day

"Orange is a color of liberation, from the pains of hurtful love and inner insecurities. To 'channel orange' is to truly be free, to be you." – Frank Ocean

Orange is generally associated with the following feelings and state of being

**Enough orange:** Lively; broad-minded; open-minded; joy; fun; sociable; energy of creation; optimistic; stimulated intellect; emotional balance; change and transformation/flexibility; healthy sexual expression; relationships; nurturing; abundance and prosperity.

**Too much orange:** Fearful; timid; shy; frivolity; lack of serious intellectual values; problems with sexuality; problems with relationships; guilt; blame; money problems.

Orange has the following physical and emotional healing properties

Frees and releases emotions; freeing action is good for relieving repressions.

Releases feelings of unworthiness, low self-esteem, self-pity and unwillingness to forgive.

Renews interest in life.

It is a natural anti-depressant (brings about changes in the biochemical structure).

Stimulates the appetite.

Relaxes muscle spasms and cramps.

Helps assimilate new ideas and stimulate mental enlightenment.

Recommended for wet coughs, sinus problems, and menstrual cramps.

Orange is not helpful in the following instances

High blood pressure

Anger and irritability

Nausea

You can use orange in your home in this way

Good for any active or creative areas. It invokes excitement and enthusiasm.

To be avoided in bedrooms or areas of high stress because of its stimulating effect.

Orange affirmations to be repeated often to help you through challenges

I feel my emotions and release them; I feel alive and well; I have a right to joy and happiness.

Orange foods

Apricots, pumpkins, carrots, mangos, saffron, nectarines, Vitamin B, calcium.

**When you wear orange**

It creates a cheerful and conscientious image.

However, too much orange can project a placid and timid nature.

**Chakra link**

Associated with the sacral chakra: The seat of loving relationships.

**Fragrances and crystals**

Orange blossom; Neroli.

Carnelian; Citrine.

**Preferences and aversions**

A preference for orange can signify a warm, sociable, dynamic and independent person; someone who dedicates themselves to whatever they do.

An aversion to orange can signify supressed sexual feelings or challenges with sensual enjoyment of life, over-sensuality, or being indulgent or too materialistic.

# 12 – Confident yellow

As you spend the day connecting to CONFIDENT YELLOW, you should feel its power in your stimulated intellect, confidence and cheerfulness.

Since yellow helps stimulate the intellect, memory and helps bring clear judgement you are going to put it to the test.

If you can, find a small mentally stimulating puzzle to do, for example a short cross word or Sudoku. Spend about five minutes working on this. Then, connect with yellow in any way you choose. You can visualize yourself in a big, yellow egg (ready to hatch? ☺), or create a beautiful space with bright yellow flowers and blankets. Even try make use of some yellow fragrances if you can. As you immerse yourself in the color, finish the rest of the mind puzzle, being very mindful of the experience and the effect of yellow around you.

Was there any difference in your clarity of thought? Was it any easier to complete the puzzle?

_____

_____

Did you feel any difference in your emotions?

_____

_____

Were you physically calmer or more energised?

_____

_____

Did you notice any changes in your body?

_____

_____

**Balanced:** Confidence; clear logical mind/mental clarity; intellect; self-esteem; personal power; warm-hearted; inspiring; wisdom; own will.

**Unbalanced:** Lack of personal power; low self-esteem; obsessive behaviour; cowardice; perfectionism.

Yellow has the following physical and emotional healing properties

Strengthens the nervous system and soothes it. It is excellent for nerve-related conditions.

Activates and cheers up depressed or melancholic people.

Connects one to the mental self and helps with the ability to perceive and understand.

Good for concentration and focus. It brings clarity of thought and new ideas.

It has an alkalising effect, as well as cleansing so is recommended in the healing of liver problems, constipation and diabetes, as well as conditions of the stomach and intestines.

Beneficial for skin problems.

Helps to dissipate judgement and criticism.

Connecting to yellow can help build self-confidence.

Yellow is not helpful for

Anyone who is too studious and analytical.

Insomniacs

Hyperactive individuals

How to use yellow in your home

Recommended for kitchens, dining rooms and bathrooms due to its energising and uplifting effect.

Helps to make small spaces feels expansive and welcoming.

A great color to use in a library or study room due to its mental stimulating effect.

If over-used in one room it's known to cause frustration and people losing their temper.

Yellow affirmations to be repeated often to help you through challenges

Ideas flow to me; I am powerful; I will.

Bananas; eggs; lemons; pineapple; cheese; yellow squash; Vitamin C; iodine; magnesium.

Alive and optimistic.

An air of charm and intelligence.

Associated with the solar plexus: The seat of self-confidence.

Lemongrass; melissa.

Citrine; topaz; amber.

A preference for yellow can signify a connection to cheerfulness, curiosity, flexibility, learning, vitality and energy.

An aversion to yellow can signify disappointment and bitterness; a tendency to rationalize feelings a tendency to avoid the depth of life by having many superficial relationships and often changing activities.

# 13 – Balanced green

As you connect to BALANCED GREEN today, expect a calm, kind, harmonious day.

*Activity*

As often as you can throughout the day, take a few moments to do a short visualization:

- Sit quietly and comfortably.
- Take three long, slow breathes, focusing on your heart as you do.
- Imagine yourself standing in a big open field, on beautiful, bright green grass.
- As you breathe in, see yourself being showered with green, so it fills your whole body, or you can imagine the green of the grass moving up through your feet and filling you.
- In your mind, expand the green out so you are surrounded by a huge circle of it.
- When you feel ready, you can open your eyes again.

What effect did the visualization have on you?

_____

_____

Did you feel any different before and after doing it? Was there any change in your mood or body?

_____

_____

Are you aware of your association to green? Do you like it/hate it?

_____

_____

Did you notice green in other place through the day? What does green mean to you?

_____

_____

Green is the prime color of the world, and that from which its loveliness arises. - Pedro Calderon

**Balanced:** Compassion; love; balance; prosperity; harmony; co-operation; curiosity; space; direction; honesty; relaxation; comfort; soothing; steady emotions; sympathy; abundance and plenty; universal healing color.

**Unbalanced:** Over-cautious; insecure; loneliness; indifference; envious and jealous.

Antiseptic properties.

Good for promoting balance, self-acceptance and compassion for self and others.

Soothing influence for the both the body and mind – brings psychological and emotional balance and harmony therefore excellent in times of stress.

It can clean and purify anything from germs, bacteria and rotting material.

Cures hormonal imbalances and stimulates growth hormone.

It can harmonize and heal almost all organs.

Helps with any heart condition, especially high blood pressure.

When in doubt, green always works.

Indecisiveness

Green can be used anywhere, but most helpful in areas used for relaxation.

Adding other colors to green will prevent total inactivity and indecision.

I have a right to love and be loved; I feel love and harmony around me; I am love.

Avocado; beans; peas; zucchini; spinach; green grapes; broccoli; green peppers; zinc; copper.

### When you wear green

You create the image of stability and efficiency.

You appear calm, controlled and at peace with the world.

### Chakra link

Linked to the heart chakra: The seat of love and compassion.

### Fragrances and crystals

Peppermint; geranium.

Bloodstone; emerald.

### Preferences and aversions

A preference for green can signify an interest in nature, plants, children and animals; a dislike of conflict; a longing for a safe home and family life.

An aversion to green can signify independence and interest in self-development as opposed to a warm family life; a preference for keeping distance in sexual relationships.

# 14 – Calming blue

Clear communication, peace, and trust are what to expect today as you associate with **CALMING BLUE.**

**Activity**

Is there something specific you need to express or communicate? Do you need to speak to someone about an issue you've been avoiding, or are you doing a public presentation? Maybe you have been wanting to express yourself by writing a book, or share an opinion you're afraid to?

Whatever your most urgent means of communication, use blue today to help you with it. Decide on one thing you can do today that has you communicating (but will push you out your comfort zone). Before you do, connect with blue. Try wearing a blue outfit, a blue scarf, or have a cup of tea with honey (yes – honey is BLUE). Notice what the color does for you, then go ahead… communicate, express, push yourself and see what happens!

How did you feel before and after connecting to the blue?

_____

_____

Did your mood change?

_____

_____

Did you notice changes in your body?

_____

_____

Where do you use blue in your life normally?

_____

_____

Do you have a preference for or aversion to blue?

_____

_____

**Blue is generally associated with the following emotions and state of being**

**Balanced:** Calm; communication; trust; peace; speaking your truth; responsibility; free expression; integrity; loyalty; inspiration; devotion; cooling; soothing; encourages creative thinking; relaxing.

**Unbalanced:** Unfaithful; superstitious; apathy; aloof and distant; criticism; addiction.

**Blue has the following physical and emotional healing properties**

Reduces inflammation.

Good for infections, especially stings and fevers, sore throats and laryngitis.

Relieves insomnia.

Soothing, calming and sedative effect makes it helpful for stress, anxiety, psychosis and obsessions.

Good for cuts, bruises and burns; anti-itching and anti-irritation.

Induces trust and decisiveness.

Helps dispel a weak will.

Enhances communication and speech.

Calms strong emotions like anger, aggression or hysteria.

**Blue is not help for**

Depression

Loneliness

**Use blue in your home**

In bedrooms for its calming, relaxing effect.

Not recommended for rooms requiring physical activity or play rooms.

A light blue in small rooms creates the feeling of spaciousness and light.

**Blue affirmations to be repeated often to help you through challenges**

I speak my truth; I am at peace; I have the right to speak and hear truth.

### Foods

Honey; milk; fish; blueberries; blue plums; oxygen; iodine; phosphorous.

### Wear blue to

Give off the feeling of versatility and tranquillity.

Create the image of patience and understanding.

Aid clear communication when you need to speak and express yourself.

### Chakra link

Linked to the throat chakra: The seat of communication.

### Fragrances and crystals

Cypress; tea tree.

Turquoise; aquamarine.

### Preferences and aversions

A preference for blue can signify dreaminess and magical; a need for peace and rest; a person who gives calm, practical advice but keeps a certain distance; someone faithful and loyal with a sense for rational thinking.

An aversion to blue can signify a disciplined, strong career worker; someone with a clear direction in life and little room for detour.

# 15 – Intuitive indigo

**Activity**

Since indigo is all about connecting to the intuition, today's activity is just that. Throughout the day, become aware of how you are making decisions. Do you agonise over every little decision, or do you JUST KNOW what to do next, even if it doesn't always make logical sense? If you JUST KNOW, it's normally your intuition speaking.

At the end of the day, pick one problem or something you have to make a decision about, even if it's small. If you can, eat some 'indigo' food (plums, red grapes, blueberries, aubergines) and connect to the indigo fragrances. Don't think about your problem too much but just ask your intuition to show you how to solve it….and then watch what happens!

(This is all your own experiment and fun with color… so no guarantees what will happen, just open to the mystery!)

How easy is it for you to connect to your intuition?

_____

_____

Did the connection to indigo help in using your intuition?

_____

_____

Did your mood or feelings change when you connected to the color?

_____

_____

**Nature's indigo inspiration to leave you with**

Look up at the night sky, revel in the stars and howl to the moon. Get new insight and know that we are not alone.

**Indigo is generally associated with the following emotions and state of being**

**Balanced:** Intuition; perception; discernment; sharp mind; perception beyond the five senses; psychic; insight; imagination; astringent; fearless; practical idealist; articulate; openness to ideas of others; emotional intelligence; ability to learn from others; devotion.

**Unbalanced**: Self-doubt; apologetic; fearful; impractical; easily depressed; scattered mind; inhibited; fanaticism; inflated ego.

**Indigo has the following physical and emotional healing properties**

Purifies the bloodstream.

Stimulates and controls the pineal gland.

Stimulates the para-thyroid and depresses the thyroid.

Powerful anaesthetic and pain reliever.

Beneficial in treating eye problems such as glaucoma and cataracts.

Helps with ear and nose complaints, as well as asthma.

Helps alleviate inhibitions and fears.

Freeing and purifying agent.

Connects one to the unconscious self.

Promotes deep concentration during meditation and introspection.

**Indigo is not helpful for**

Addictions or workaholics as it may aggravate addictive behaviour.

Anyone feeling "spaced out".

**Use indigo in your home**

In private rooms and bedrooms.

**Indigo affirmations to be repeated often to help you through challenges**

I see the truth; I can trust myself; I am open to imagine.

**Foods**

Plums; aubergines; beetroot; blue grapes; Vitamin K.

**Wearing indigo**

Can make you appear individualistic and possibly radical.

Shows you may be unconventional, but interested in new ideas and people.

**Chakra link**

Link to third eye chakra: The seat of intuition.

**Fragrances and crystals**

Jasmine; chamomile.

Lapis lazuli; sodalite.

**Preferences and aversions**

A preference for indigo can signify someone who is idealistic, searching for harmony and warm intimacy.

An aversion to indigo can signify someone who is overcautious, argumentative and a strong ego.

# 16 – Spiritual violet

Today, open yourself up to the **SPIRITUAL** and transformative nature of VIOLET.

## Activity

It's simple for today – put on your most violet outfit and meditate in whatever way you choose (or just be still). Surrender and enjoy!

Do you feel a connection to violet?

_____

_____

Did you feel inspired to mediate wearing it? Was there any difference to your meditation practice? Was it easy to be still?

_____

_____

Is violet a color you resonate with? Do you have it anywhere in your home – if so, how does that room feel?

_____

_____

**Here's what Leonardo Da Vinci proclaimed about violet**

You can increase the power of meditation ten-fold by meditating under the gentle rays of violet, as found in church windows.

**Violet is generally associated with the following emotions and state of being**

**Balanced:** Spirituality; loyalty; vision; transformation; surrender; selflessness; ethics; inspiration; dignity; creative arts – music and art; humanitarians.

**Unbalanced:** Martyrdom; self-sacrifice; pretentious; conceited; arrogance; superiority.

**Violet has the following physical and emotional healing properties**

Stimulates the pituitary gland – the master gland of the endocrine system.

Gives energy to the lymphatic system.

Can heal melancholy and hysteria.

Helps with immunity by stimulating the spleen and white blood cells.

Enhances purpose and dignity.

Encourages introspection.

Connects one the to the spiritual self and brings guidance, wisdom and inner strength.

Enhances any meditation practice.

**Violet is not helpful**

If someone is too introspective.

Nightmares

Addictions

**Use violet in your home**

In libraries and study rooms. It helps with concentration and focus.

It gives a room depth.

Light violet like lavender brings a restful quality to bedrooms without it feeling cool.

**Violet affirmations to be repeated often to help you through challenges**

I can transform negativity; I am connected to my highest self; I have power and use it wisely.

**Foods**

Currants/raisins; olives; blackberries; vitamin D; potassium.

**Wearing violet**

Creates an image of an unconventional nature and an idealist.

Portrays one as a unique thinker.

Will encourage mystery, imagination and spirituality.

**Chakra link**

Linked to the crown chakra: The seat of connection to your source.

**Fragrances and crystals**

Lavender; frankincense.

Amethyst; lepidolite.

**Preferences and aversions**

A preference to violet can signify a longing to improve the world and ascend; being characterized by mystery and dignity; a soft, sensitive nature; someone with paranormal abilities.

An aversion to violet can signify a serious attitude towards life; no place for dreams or fantasies; a rejection of anything unnatural or unrealistic.

# 17 – Pretty pink

It's time to get in touch with your feminine side with today's focus on **PRETTY PINK.**

## Activity

Pink is the color of unconditional love.

Today, become super observant of pink everywhere: See how it is used in the media, do a google search for pink logos and see what comes up, try find and eat pink foods.

What is your association with pink?

_____

_____

Do you have an attraction or aversion to it?

_____

_____

How does your body react when you see or think of pink? What thoughts, feelings or emotions come up?

_____

_____

**In the spirit of pink and unconditional love, this is what the actress Audrey Hepburn had to say**

I believe in pink.

**Pink is generally associated with the following emotions and state of being**

**Balanced:** Warmth; nurturing; unconditional love; softness; tenderness; caring; romance; youthful; friendship; femininity; emotional healing; hope.

**Unbalanced:** Emotionally draining; physical weakness; over-cautious; over-emotional; naïve; lack of will power.

**Pink has the following physical and emotional healing properties**

Stimulates the immune system.

Alleviates insomnia.

Reduces erratic behaviour, irritation and aggression.

Stimulates the heart, heartbeat and raises blood pressure.

Helps in the healing of stress, trauma, anger and aggression.

Relieves feelings of loneliness, oversensitivity and vulnerability.

Heals grief and sadness.

Restores youthfulness.

Helps bring one in contact with feelings.

**Pink is not helpful**

An overdose can create physical weakness.

Increasing physical energy.

**Use pink in your home**

Good for baby and children's bedrooms because of the soothing, loving properties.

Avoid in physical activity rooms where great physical energy is required.

**Pink affirmations to be repeated often to help you through challenges**

I am calm; I lovingly accept all parts of myself; I give love openly.

**Foods**

Salmon; grapefruit.

**Wear pink to**

Create a softer, feminine feel.

Present yourself as non-threatening, calm and peaceful.

**Chakra link**

Pink can also be associated with the heart chakra: The seat of unconditional love.

**Fragrances and crystals**

Rose; peony; grapefruit.

Rose quartz; pink sapphire; rhodonite.

**Preferences and aversions**

A preference for pink can signify femininity, a sweet, soft, innocent nature; people who are kind and tender.

An aversion to pink can signify someone who struggles to express tenderness and emotions. An avoidance of the feminine aspect of themselves.

# 18 – Rebelling black

**BLACK** is about rebelling, but also about protection and breaking free from bad habits – see how it works for you.

## Activity

Everyone has black in their cupboards.

Today, dress in all black – no color whatsoever (if you have rock star tendencies, this should be no problem at all!). The focus is for you to become aware of how you feel, but mostly how your personal interactions and relations are through the day.

Remember for any of these activities there is no right or wrong, it's all about observing and enjoying your own experiments with color.

Was it easy or difficult for you to dress in all black?

_____

_____

How did you feel throughout the day?

_____

_____

Did people react any differently to you?

_____

_____

Were you aware of any changes in your personal space? Did you feel any more protected?

_____

_____

**In parting today, here are some color quotes on black**

There's something about black, you feel hidden away in it. - Georgia O'Keefe

I'll stop wearing black when they invent a darker color. - Anonymous

Black is modest and arrogant at the same time. Black is lazy and easy – but mysterious. But above all, black says this, 'I don't bother you – don't bother me.' - Yohji Yamamoto

**Black is generally associated with the following emotions and state of being**

**Balanced:** Protection; mystery; silence; infinite; authoritative; powerful; control; contained; strong.

**Unbalanced:** Prevents one from growing and changing; isolation; excessive mourning; depressive; overwhelming; emptiness; intimidating; secretive.

**Black has the following physical and emotional healing properties**

Can help in breaking free from bad habits or addictions.

Promotes liberation, strength and self-discipline.

Protects one from negative influences or energy.

**Black is not helpful for**

Excessive depression.

**Use black in your home**

It will enhance the energy of another color in a room – grounding it and giving it depth.

Good for creating space for reflection and inner searching.

**Black affirmations to be repeated often to help you through challenges**

I am safe and protected; I am strong; I dispel all negativity.

**Foods**

Black tea; black pepper; liquorice.

**Wearing black**

Projects a feeling of mystery.

Recommended if one needs to feel protected.

Worn in excess can cut one off from connection and communication.

Creates a thinner, sophisticated look.

**Chakra link**

No specific link

**Fragrances and crystals**

Anise; liquorice.

Black tourmaline; hematite.

**Preferences and aversions**

A preference for black can signify seriousness; depression; a need to stand apart and/or revolt against the norm; a need to revolt against one's fate; the need to keep your energy protected; someone who trusts themselves explicitly; someone who is extreme – all or nothing.

An aversion to black can signify a fear of the unknown; fear of the abuse of power; a desire to become free from all kinds of dependency and blockages.

# 19 – Earthly brown and Neutral grey

This chapter is different as we'll explore two colors in one – **EARTHLY BROWN** is about stability and NEUTRAL GREY all about neutrality, but be open to what they each mean to you.

## Activity

Get back into nature.

If you can, dig in the dirt, plant something, find some "pet rocks" (brown and grey - you might like to name them). As much as you can, spend time barefoot. This is especially good if you can find some fresh soil or dark brown sand. If you're the complete city slicker, think out the box; and try find a playground with a sandpit. And as much as you can, become aware of grey in nature.

How did it feel to connect to the earthiness of brown?

_____

_____

What feelings came up for you around grey?

_____

_____

Do these colors resonate with you? How do they affect your mood?

_____

_____

Do you wear these colors often?

_____

_____

Remember a color isn't just a color, there are kaleidoscopes of shades and tints. Here's some fun names you can come across when it comes to different types of brown and grey:

| | |
|---|---|
| **Mocha** | Ash |
| **Chocolate** | Charcoal |
| **Chestnut** | Cool |
| **Tan** | Slate |
| **Carmel** | Timberwolf |

**Brown is generally associated with the following emotions and state of being**

**Brown balanced:** Earth; stable; grounding; conservation; protection; warm; serious; down-to-earth; support; structure; belonging; material security; honesty; sincerity.

**Brown unbalanced:** Depressing; frugal; dull; lack of humour; predictable; stingy.

**Grey is generally associated with the following emotions and state of being**

**Grey balanced:** Neutral; neutralising; independence; self-reliant; protection from outside influence.

**Grey unbalanced:** Unsettling; creates expectations; narrow mindedness; repressed emotions; lack of self-worth; indifferent; non-expressive; non-committal; suppressive.

**Brown has the following physical and emotional healing properties**

Brings stability and alleviates insecurity.

Can be used to create a safe haven.

Reassures and comforts.

Encourages order and organization.

It encourages material security.

Helps with grounding and creates a connection to the earth.

Gives a feeling of wholesomeness.

Helps maintain neutrality and detachment.

Encourages objectivity.

Some light grey can be soothing and calming.

Helps if compromise is required.

## Brown is not helpful for

Depression

Materialistic individuals

## Grey is not helpful for

Sadness

Isolation

## Home use

### Brown

A good, grounding accessory color – too much can be overpowering.

### Grey

As an accessory color it can be calming and soothing.

## Brown affirmations to be repeated often to help you through challenges

I belong; I am safe and provided for; I am always supported.

## Grey affirmations to be repeated often to help you through challenges

I do not react; I remain calm and detached.

## Brown foods

Chocolate; cocoa; whole-wheat bread; coffee; nuts.

Oysters; mushrooms.

**Wear brown to:**

Project an image of a practical, stable individual.

Help you stay neutral and hide your true nature.

It produces the image of being neutral.

Suggests efficiency but also lack of imagination and initiative.

**Chakra link**

**Brown**

Earth star chakra

Grey

No chakra links

**Fragrances and crystals**

**Brown**

Nutmeg; cinnamon; almond.

Tiger's Eye; petrified wood.

Grey

No specific scents.

Hematite; galena.

## Preferences and aversions

### Brown

A preference for brown can signify a strong need for security; practical people. A preference for natural, tribal things; solidity and simplify.

An aversion for brown can signify a disregard for the earth and one's body; an aversion to normal, everyday life; disconnection from one's home/family; instability in health.

### Grey

A preference for grey can signify a neutral, indifferent person; non-expressive; someone who is lifeless, fixed and apathetic; reserved, cool people; an unwillingness to expose oneself.

An aversion to grey can signify someone who prefers to be straight to the point; knowing where on stands; a need for clarity; an aversion to political or tactical attitudes.

# 20 – Make your new color consciousness work for you

Wow, that's Become Color Conscious almost done! By now I hope the world seems a more fun, delightful place, and at least more COLORFUL!

All that's left is for you to now integrate everything you have been awakened to – in a practical, experiential way.

Although you've been experimenting with color every day already, the next two chapters are about considering everything you have learnt and applying it to ONE aspect of your life or problem that needs some healing or change. Consider it a secret color mission.

## FINAL COLOR MISSION...

1. Choose one issue in your life that is out of balance, a specific problem, or something you want to heal (it could be physical, mental, emotional, relationship, spiritual). If there's not one specific thing, you can also just focus on an area of your life you have never made color a part of, but want to try enhance through color.

2. Your mission is to improve this situation/problem, or try balance/heal by applying your new color consciousness. Consider all the ways color can be applied and how you have personally responded to different colors and activities after the last 18 chapters and try find a new, creative way of applying color so it does result in a positive change.

For the confused of you out there, here's an example:

I have been struggling with low iron levels, which means low energy and poor physical performance.

Since red is about energy and relates to the blood, I made a point of wearing red when I went for my last run to see how if it would make any difference. Being very conscious during my run, I observed my energy, and could also measure how far and fast I was running.

Such a great surprise – I felt stronger, my speed improved and I was able to recover much quicker.

3. You'll be doing this over the next two chapters so you have time to "play" and enjoy the experience. Make notes, get creative, throw color parties – just go wild with color!

# 21 – Make your new color consciousness work for you

How have you applied color to your problem/focus area?

_____

_____

Have you noticed any change or differences? Have you considered your emotions, moods, physical sensations or personal interactions in your evaluation?

_____

_____

Have your perceptions changed in any way after having to apply color?

_____

_____

How hard/easy was it to complete this mission?

_____

_____

Today make sure you write a short blog piece that describes your experience during this color mission.

My color mission has taught me:

My most valuable insight:

From now on, I will see the world:

# 22 – You are now color conscious

Well done! You are now color conscious!

The new color conscious you, armed with rainbows of color, ready to take on the world in a happier, healthier and more inspired light (I hope just a little at least)!

Just before you do, there's one last thing to do… your final, final color mission!

## FINAL FINAL COLOR MISSION...

Remember the pictures you took of yourself, or created, back on day 1?

Your last task is to re-do this.
So re-take a picture of yourself or re-do an artistic impression, and paste it here.

Now go back to the one from chapter 1 and compare.
Do you look different?

_____

_____

Is there a focus on different colors? What color would you describe yourself as now?

_____

_____

Do you feel you could use a certain color for balance – is it different from what you said in chapter 1?

_____

_____

_____

What mood or emotions does your picture display?

_____

_____

_____

_____

# Afterword

Thank you for doing (red), having the courage (orange), focussing (yellow), sharing (green), posting (blue), connecting (indigo), and becoming conscious (violet). You have made me the happiest Chick Rainbow Chick (my Twitter name @chicrainbowchik) in the universe. My wish is that you go out and spread the amazing word of color.

Printed in the United States
By Bookmasters